American Life and Video Games from Pong to Minecraft

KATHRYN HULICK

Cavendish
Square

New York

Published in 2017 by Cavendish Square Publishing, LLC
243 5th Avenue, Suite 136, New York, NY 10016

Copyright © 2017 by Cavendish Square Publishing, LLC

First Edition

Website: cavendishsq.com

This publication represents the opinions and views of the author based on his or her personal experience, knowledge,
and research. The information in this book serves as a general guide only. The author and publisher have used their best
efforts in preparing this book and disclaim liability rising directly or indirectly from the use and application of this book.

CPSIA Compliance Information: Batch #CS16CSQ

All websites were available and accurate when this book was sent to press.

Library of Congress Cataloging-in-Publication Data

Names: Hulick, Kathryn, author.
Title: American life and video games from Pong to Minecraft / Kathryn Hulick.
Description: New York : Cavendish Square Publishing, 2017. |
Series: Pop culture. | Includes bibliographical references and index.
Identifiers: LCCN 2016000272 (print) | LCCN 2016012677 (ebook) |
ISBN 9781502619754 (library bound) | ISBN 9781502619761 (ebook)
Subjects: LCSH: Video games--Social aspects--United States--Juvenile literature. |
Video games--History--Juvenile literature.
Classification: LCC GV1469.34.S52 H85 2017 (print) | LCC GV1469.34.S52 (ebook) |
DDC 794.8--dc23
LC record available at http://lccn.loc.gov/2016000272

Editorial Director: David McNamara
Editor: Kelly Spence
Copy Editor: Nathan Heidelberger
Art Director: Jeffrey Talbot
Designer: Jessica Nevins
Production Assistant: Karol Szymczuk
Photo Research: J8 Media

Printed in the United States of America

Contents

Introduction

THE URGE TO PLAY GAMES IS AN ESSENTIAL part of human nature. Pretend play, board games, card games, and sports have been around since ancient times. Video games enhance the age-old gaming experience through technology, employing sound effects, **graphics**, and entire **virtual** worlds. The rise of video games followed closely on the heels of the computer age. Over the decades since the end of World War II (1939–1945), computers have transformed from gigantic, obscure machines that only academics understood to small, sleek devices that anyone can carry in his or her pocket.

A person needs both extra spending money and free time in order to play video games, making this popular pastime a marker of **prosperity**. Most video games have been developed in the United States and Japan, which are among the world's richest nations. Dedicated **game consoles** such as the PlayStation or Xbox have always been expensive

Opposite: Video gaming is a major entertainment industry. Today, many people enjoy playing games such as *Candy Crush Saga* on mobile devices.

luxury items. But as laptops, tablets, and especially cell phones become cheaper and more widely available, a growing number of people from all economic backgrounds now have access to video games. Not only can they play games, they can play together in large online communities, thanks to the Internet and wireless technology. Through video games, people have made friends in other countries and have even fallen in love with people they met in gaming worlds.

Video games mix together many traditional art forms, including painting, writing, music, and movie-making, in order to engage audiences. Like these art forms, games reflect current events and social movements. Over the decades, the "bad guys" in some video games have mirrored the enemies in real wars, from the Nazis of World War II to **communists** during the Cold War to terrorists today. Representations of minorities, women, and homosexuals in games have also evolved as these segments of the population have campaigned for equality.

The advent of gamer culture has changed the United States. During the 1990s and early 2000s, many gamers were social outcasts labeled as "geeks" or "nerds" who found a feeling of kinship and belonging among their like-minded peers. As the popularity of video games spread and the Internet made communication among gamers easier, they formed online communities. As these communities grew, they found ways to get together and share their love of games in the real world, gathering at conventions such as PAX, an annual event started in 2004. Today, gamers also compete in elite gaming competitions that offer cash awards and fame to the top players.

By the 2010s, technology was everywhere—and it was cool. People of all ages and both genders were playing games. Businesses turned to "gamification" as a marketing tool to increase engagement with their customers. To gamify a process or a product, a company adds **game mechanics** such as the ability to earn points or unlock content. Gradually, the labels "geek" and "nerd" lost their negative meanings.

Video games offer players entire virtual worlds to explore and the opportunity to become whomever they want. A person who had never excelled at sports can score the winning touchdown. An overweight person can play a lithe, muscular hero. A person without any influence in the real world can rule over a fantasy realm.

Today, video games are an inescapable part of a culture in which virtual worlds and virtual selves are increasingly intertwined with reality.

1950s:

Dawn of the Computer Age

MOST AMERICANS FONDLY REMEMBER THE 1950s as a time of prosperity. Perhaps this decade seemed sunnier following on the heels of World War II. Considered to be the deadliest conflict in history, the war brought six long years of brutal fighting that killed millions of people. European countries suffered the most casualties, but many Americans also lost their lives. Many popular video games today place players in the role of soldiers in combat. These video game characters must hunt down their enemies while avoiding gunfire, bombs, and other deadly attacks. During World War II, this type of experience was all too real.

As soldiers faced off on the battlefields of World War II, scientists and engineers on both sides raced to develop technologies and weapons that would outsmart or out-gun the enemy. If not for the war, many things we take for granted today may have been developed much later or not at all. Major wartime inventions included plastics, nuclear

Opposite: This Bombe machine helped the British crack enemy codes during World War II. These code-breaking efforts spurred the development of computer technology.

power, and radar. Machines that were forerunners to the first computers were also developed during World War II. This computer technology later made video games possible. However, games wouldn't become available to the general public until the 1970s. Computers are such an integral part of our daily life now that it is almost impossible to remember a time when this technology did not exist.

CODE BREAKERS

Some of the earliest computer-like machines helped soldiers communicate in code—or crack their enemy's codes. The Enigma was a machine that Germany used to scramble secret messages in order to send them between their forces. Mathematicians in England countered with a machine called the Bombe that could decipher the secret German codes for use in Allied counterattacks. The man who invented the Bombe also cracked other important wartime codes. His name was Alan Turing.

Alan Turing helped create the field of computer science.

Many consider Alan Turing the father of computer science. He envisioned a modern computer in 1936—long before one had been built—and called it a Universal Turing Machine. His innovative design introduced the idea of **computer programming.** A person could feed the machine a step-by-step procedure, then the computer would use that procedure to solve a problem. Turing was also one of the first people to propose the idea that computers can think and learn, a concept now known as **artificial intelligence.** He even started working on a program to play the game of checkers.

Turing predicted that a computer could probably learn to play "very good chess." In 1997, the computer program Deep Blue beat world chess champion Garry Kasparov. Intelligent computer programs have also defeated humans at checkers, *Jeopardy!*, and some forms of poker. Today, artificial intelligence lurks behind the scenes in many popular video games.

A TRAGIC END

Alan Turing's brilliant code breaking helped the Allies win World War II. However, even his heroic efforts couldn't save him from prejudice. Turing was gay, and in the 1950s, homosexuality was illegal in Britain. After Turing's relationship with a younger man was discovered, he was convicted in 1952. He died two years later, at the age of forty-two. It is believed by many that he committed suicide. The British government officially pardoned Turing in 2013.

A GIANT MACHINE

Today, you can slip a computer into your pocket or wear one in your glasses. In 1946, the only fully electronic computer in the world took up an entire room. ENIAC weighed about 30 tons (27.2 metric tons)—as much as five elephants. At the time, the word "computer" was not yet used for this massive machine. Instead, the word referred to a human, often a woman, who performed calculations.

Believe it or not, the wall of switches behind this operator is just the main control panel of the gigantic ENIAC computer.

The American mathematician John von Neumann further developed Turing's ideas and joined John Mauchly, John Eckert, and a team of engineers working to put these ideas to work in the world's first computer. Named the Electronic Numerical Integrator and Computer, or ENIAC, the computer started out as a secret wartime project at the Moore School of Electrical Engineering at the University of Pennsylvania. The US government planned to use the machine to perform calculations needed for firing missiles. However, the war ended before the computer was completed. In February 1946, the team announced ENIAC to the public. The computer age had officially begun.

AMERICAN PROSPERITY

The race to produce enough weapons and material goods for the war effort boosted the American economy, ushering in a decade of wealth and consumerism. Wages were rising and many items that had been hard to find during the war became available. Americans purchased millions of new cars, televisions, refrigerators, vacuum cleaners, and other luxuries of the modern age. They settled in the suburbs and began shopping at malls and eating fast food—the first McDonald's opened in 1955. They also started families. So many children were born between 1946 and 1964 that historians refer to the trend as a "baby boom." During this time, society generally expected that the father would work while the mother stayed home and cared for the house and children. Middle-class families regularly watched TV together or went to the movies. Video games as a family pastime did not yet exist.

THE FIRST VIDEO GAMES

While many American families enjoyed the economic boom, academics and engineers in the United States and Europe

During the 1950s, consumerism reigned. Purchasing a new television, car, or refrigerator was a marker of prosperity.

were continuing to develop computer technology. Some of these academics started experimenting with games. Scientists in Britain designed some of the first computer games to show off the capabilities of these new machines. In 1951, a festival celebrating science introduced the Nimrod computer, which had been specially designed to play the game nim. In this old-fashioned game, players pick up matches from piles. The player to pick up the last match wins. As its display, the computer used a grid of fixed lights that turned on and off to represent the matches. Other early games included a version of tic-tac-toe, called *OXO*, created by A. S. Douglas in 1952. A few years later, Arthur Samuel built on Turing's earlier ideas to write the first checkers-playing program. It was demonstrated on television in 1956, and in 1962, it beat a human opponent.

However, none of these early games involved moving graphics. Many consider *Tennis for Two* (1958) to be the first real video game. *Tennis for Two* was invented at Brookhaven National Laboratory in Long Island, New York. There, scientists needed a way to demonstrate what computers could do while also entertaining visitors at an upcoming open house. William Higinbotham came up with a brilliant idea: he made a tennis game. Visitors loved it! The game was displayed on an oscilloscope, a small device with a tiny, 5-inch- (12.7-centimeter-) wide screen that usually displayed electric voltage. For the demonstration, the screen showed a bouncing ball. Players used controllers to knock it back and forth in a virtual tennis match. Higinbotham later wrote about his invention: "It might liven up the place to have a game that

At Brookhaven National Laboratory in 1958, people lined up to try out a groundbreaking video game called *Tennis for Two*, shown here.

people could play, and which would convey the message that our scientific endeavors have relevance for society."

THE DECADE IN REVIEW

Brookhaven National Laboratory set up *Tennis for Two* two years in a row at their annual open house, but that was all. Only people who happened to visit the open house knew about it. The rest of the world remained largely unaware that computers could be used to play games. However, Higinbotham was certainly correct that advances in science affect society as a whole. Often, the way new technology changes culture is impossible to predict. The advent of computer technology starting in the 1950s has had perhaps the most profound impact on daily life today. Almost every device in people's lives today has a computer in it somewhere—from cell phones, kitchen appliances, cameras, and cars to video game consoles. In the 1950s, Higinbotham never could have guessed that by the turn of the century, video games would become a billion-dollar industry.

TWO

1960s:
The Space Race

THE 1960S WAS A DECADE FRAUGHT WITH protests as people clamored for social change. The civil rights movement campaigned for rights for black people. The feminist movement aimed to place women on equal footing with men. Protests against the Vietnam War called for peace and an end to a bloody conflict taking place in Southeast Asia. Young people played important roles in all of these movements. The decade also began with the 1960 election of America's youngest president: John F. Kennedy. He was just forty-three years old. Under the Kennedy administration, for a brief time the United States was considered akin to Camelot, the mythical and peaceful home of King Arthur and his knights.

However, that peace was shattered in 1963 when an assassin shot and killed Kennedy as he rode in an open car through the streets of Dallas, Texas. Across the United States, people followed the tragedy on national television. In 1968, another prominent leader was assassinated: Martin Luther King Jr., the influential spokesman for the civil rights movement. King was a Baptist minister who preached nonviolent protest. His words inspired a generation of people of all races to find peaceful ways to work toward social change.

Despite these tragedies, a rising crime rate, and violence that inevitably broke out during the decade's many protests, technology continued to advance. The space race inspired the nation and gave rise to a huge variety of space-themed television shows, movies, and eventually video games.

BLAST OFF

"That's one small step for man, one giant leap for mankind." Neil Armstrong spoke these famous words on July 20, 1969, as he stepped onto the surface of the moon. This milestone marked the culmination of the space race between the United States and the Soviet Union. The two nations had begun racing one another into outer space in the late 1950s while involved in a conflict known as the Cold War. This conflict pitted the democratic United States against the communist Soviet Union. Each side sought to prove its superiority in ideology, weaponry, and technology.

Neil Armstrong and Buzz Aldrin, shown here, became the first two people to walk on the surface of the moon. This historic achievement was part of the Apollo 11 mission.

The space race blasted off in 1957, when the Soviet Union launched *Sputnik 1*, the first human-made object to orbit the Earth. This launch alarmed many Americans, who worried that the Soviet Union might use this technology to bomb the United States. In response, the US government founded the National Aeronautics and Space Administration, better known as NASA, in 1958. In 1961, Russian cosmonaut Yuri Gagarin became the first person in space. The United States sent Alan Shepard into space just a few months later. President Kennedy then declared that the United States would aim to send a person to the moon by the end of the decade. While Kennedy didn't live to see his goal become a reality, hundreds of millions of people around the world tuned in to watch the historic moon landing on television.

SPACEWAR!

Americans loved the exotic, futuristic idea of space travel. It's not surprising that space worked its way into popular culture in television shows, music, movies, books, and art. The television series *Star Trek* (1966–1969) and the movie *2001: A Space Odyssey* (1968) each imagined what the future might hold for space travel. Science fiction novels set in space rose in popularity through the 1960s, and singer David Bowie released "Space Oddity" in 1969. Space also provided the spark for an early video game: *Spacewar!* (1962).

Steve Russell was a student at the Massachusetts Institute of Technology (MIT) who had access to a powerful new computer. He came up with the game as a way to show off what the machine could do. In *Spacewar!*, two players attempted to destroy one another's spaceships while flying around a large star. The star's gravity could suck in and destroy spaceships if the players weren't careful. A spaceship could also fly through hyperspace, which transported the ship to a random place on

Mouse in the Maze

Spacewar! wasn't the first computer game developed at MIT. In 1959, a group of students made a game called *Mouse in the Maze*. Players would first draw a maze on the screen using a light pen, an early precursor of the computer mouse. Squares inside the maze represented cheese. Another square blob, the mouse, would move through the maze and attempt to reach the cheese.

the screen. Unfortunately, access to a computer was required in order to play. At the time, the only people who used these expensive new machines tended to be scientists, engineers, academics, and some university students. Russell gave *Spacewar!*

The PDP-1 computer made it easier for people and computers to interact. Students at MIT developed and shared early video games for the machine, including *Spacewar!*

away to anyone who wanted it. The popular game quickly spread through universities and research laboratories.

One university student who played *Spacewar!* was named Nolan Bushnell. He developed a version of the game that could be played on a coin-operated machine in an **arcade**. Named *Computer Space*, this was one of the first arcade video games. Unfortunately, the game never caught on—it was too complicated for the average player—but Bushnell didn't give up. The video game industry is lucky that he decided to try again, because Bushnell and his partner Ted Dabney went on to develop *Pong* (1972). *Pong* quickly became a sensation, making video games a part of popular culture for the first time.

GALAXY Game

Computer Space wasn't the only arcade version of *Spacewar!* Another version was installed on the campus of Stanford University in 1971. This game actually included a **computer processor**. It cost ten cents a game or twenty-five cents for three games. Bill Pitts, a Stanford graduate, teamed up with high-school friend Hugh Tuck to build the machines. They used the name *Galaxy Game* instead of *Spacewar!* because the Vietnam War protests were still in full swing. Putting the word "war" into the name of the game could have attracted negative attention. *Galaxy Game* never caught on off the Stanford campus.

PLAYING WITH TELEVISION

The early games of nim and checkers, as well as *OXO, Tennis for Two,* and *Spacewar!,* all had their roots in computer science. But another form of technology also had gaming potential:

the television. Inventor and television engineer Ralph Baer realized that the TV sets in people's homes could be used to play games. He jotted down notes for a "game box" in 1966 that could attach to any TV set and allow people to play simple games such as tennis or target shooting. By 1968, he had built a prototype, which he called the Brown Box. However, it took four more years to bring the new product to market. Finally, the game box was released in 1972 as the Magnavox Odyssey. Although not a cultural sensation, the Odyssey made its mark as the first home game system. The table tennis game on the Odyssey would help inspire the later game *Pong*.

Ralph Baer shows off a prototype of his invention: the world's first video game console system.

THE FATHER OF VIDEO GAMES

Ralph Baer earned the nickname the "father of video games" for his pioneering work on the Magnavox Odyssey. The Odyssey came with twelve games, including *Table Tennis*, *Hockey*, and *Simon Says*. Players would place translucent color overlays on the television screen to create a backdrop for the game. The system also included physical dice, poker chips, and play money. Consumers could separately purchase plastic rifles to play shooting games.

PINBALL WIZARDS

A coin-operated pinball machine was a common sight in a bar or pub during the 1930s and 1940s. Many states banned these machines, considering them a form of gambling. This forbidden status likely made the games even more attractive to young people. In the 1950s, pinball fever swept across the United States. Young people spent hours plugging coins into the machines and competing for high scores. The popularity of pinball during the 1950s, 1960s, and early 1970s was memorialized in music and TV. The rock album *Tommy* (1969) by The Who featured the hit song "Pinball Wizard," and the character Fonzie from the TV show *Happy Days* (1974–1984) often played pinball.

Starting in the 1960s, companies began developing electromechanical arcade games. These games did not use computer processors or monitors, but they did incorporate motors, switches, lights, and other electrical parts. Pinball machines started including electronic components such as a clock counter to keep score. The Japanese company Sega, which would later develop video games, released a hugely successful electromechanical game called *Periscope* (1966). These games were all important precursors to the arcade video games soon to arrive.

THE DECADE IN REVIEW

The 1960s saw video games begin to develop along three paths, based on the machines used to play the game: a computer, television set, or arcade table. These separate forms of video gaming would remain distinct throughout the coming decades. Computer games benefitted from the fact that programming allowed for incredible freedom and creativity. Most of the first video games were developed for computers as early programmers experimented with these powerful new machines. However, only people with access to computers could create or play these games. This type of gaming gradually rose in popularity as computers dropped in price and became more widely available.

The Magnavox Odyssey brought the first games into people's homes via their televisions, but home gaming wouldn't take off until the late 1970s with the Atari 2600. These systems became known as "video game consoles." Atari paved the way for the Nintendo Entertainment System (NES) in the 1980s and eventually the Sony PlayStation, Microsoft Xbox, and Nintendo Wii.

Finally, arcade video games built on the success of mechanical table games such as pinball. Pinball machines still exist today and often incorporate a screen to display graphics and the score, but the actual game still uses a real table and real balls. In contrast, an arcade video game such as *Pong* displays entirely on a screen. The player uses virtual paddles to whack a ball that is represented by a moving point of light. However, the style of early arcade game play and

Pinball machines are still popular today but are not the main attraction at arcades as they once were. Video games have taken over!

the look of the machines followed directly from mechanical games. For example, in many video games, a player starts with three lives. In pinball, players almost always get three balls to start. In both types of game, it's possible to earn extra lives or balls. Arcade video game fever would not reach the general public until the 1970s.

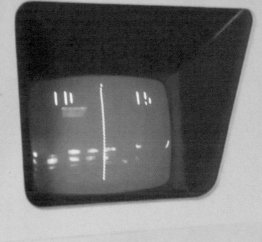

THREE

1970s:
Arcade Fever

BLIP, BLIP, BLIP, BUZZ. THESE SOUNDS
ushered in a new form of entertainment. The year was 1972,
and the game was *Pong*. It was very simple: two vertical lines
on each side of the screen represented table tennis rackets.
The ball was a small, square dot. Two players knocked the
ball back and forth. When a player missed the ball, his or her
opponent scored a point. *Pong* started a craze that brought
video games into mainstream culture.

During the 1970s, video games and other forms of
entertainment provided a welcome distraction from a
variety of crises, including high unemployment, **inflation**,
and a political scandal that led to president Richard Nixon's
resignation in 1974. Now known as Watergate, the scandal
involved Republicans breaking into a hotel to spy on Democrats
and then covering up their actions. The Vietnam War finally
ended in 1973. That same year, Americans had to deal with a
gasoline shortage after Middle Eastern nations stopped selling

Opposite: *Pong* was a simple but addictive game for two players.

oil to the United States. This was also the decade in which increasing air and water pollution forced Americans to pay more attention to how human activities could affect the planet. Americans celebrated the first Earth Day on April 22, 1970, and the government passed laws intended to help protect the environment. In the midst of all these events, people still found time to play games.

The 1970s was a decade of important firsts for this brand-new pastime, including the first arcade video games in 1971, the first home game system in 1972, and the first handheld games in 1976. The first computers that were cheap enough and small enough for people to use at home also came out during this decade, including the first personal computer in 1975. Many people thought video games would be a passing fad, like the pet rock. This gag gift became extremely popular in 1975, but people soon lost interest. Video games, however, were here to stay.

THE "ME DECADE"

The 1970s came to be known as "the me decade." The all-American ideal of a family composed of a married mother and father with two or three children had begun to fall apart in the 1960s. Through the 1970s, people continued to challenge traditional views of the family and gender roles. Divorce rates rose, the women's movement continued to campaign for equal rights and independence for women, and the gay rights movement gained steam, leading up to the National March on Washington in 1979. Young people experienced more freedom in their sexual relationships as the birth control pill became widespread. Movies and television began to feature characters and situations that would have seemed out of place or even immoral in earlier decades, including gay men, single working women, and unmarried people living together.

In addition, some people turned away from traditional religions and toward other forms of spiritual and personal fulfillment, including cults. These religious groups typically required members to abandon their normal lives and follow a spiritual leader. The new age movement also attracted attention. New age spirituality placed an emphasis on enlightenment and finding one's true self.

Young Americans also turned to new, outrageous fashions to express themselves and their individuality. Teens wore brightly colored pants called bell-bottoms that flared into huge openings around the feet. Young men grew their hair,

In 1977, arcades and afros were everywhere.

beards, and sideburns long, and both women and men strutted around in tall platform shoes. The afro, a poufy, prominent hairstyle, became popular among young black people. All of these fashion trends made an individual stand out in a crowd. Video games in the 1970s fit right in with the "me" mentality. Many early arcade games challenged a single player to test himself or herself to beat the high score.

CORRUPTING THE YOUTH

While young people sought to find themselves and then express their newfound individualities, many Americans still clung to traditional values. These people began to make their voices heard in the conservative political movement. They spoke out against government involvement in people's lives, including high taxes, environmental laws, and affirmative action laws that sought to give minorities equal opportunities in education and the workplace. Lawmakers introduced affirmative action to deal with unfair hiring practices. Despite the efforts of the civil rights movement and the feminist movement, many companies in the 1970s still tended to prefer white male candidates over equally qualified candidates of other races or genders. Some conservatives argued that affirmative action was an unfair intrusion of government into private businesses, and that qualified white male candidates would now become the targets of discrimination. Many conservatives also denounced depictions of violence, sexuality, and immoral behavior in movies, television shows, and rock music.

One video game attracted negative attention as well. In the 1970s, games could only display simple graphics in a few colors, but the arcade game *Death Race* (1976) still provoked outrage. The goal of the game was to run over stick figures called gremlins with a car. The gremlins shrieked when they died, and then a cross appeared. CNN questioned the violence in the game on national television in a *60 Minutes* segment. The National Safety Council also spoke out against the game, explaining that a video game requires the player to act out violence, which they considered worse than simply watching violence on TV or in a movie. Many arcades removed the game after the backlash. The debate about violence in games would revive again and again over the coming decades.

MEET ME AT THE ARCADE

Whether or not video games actually provoke violence or aggression is still an open question. What is certain is that games draw people in. While most people typically read a book or watch a movie just once, they play the same games again and again and again, trying to earn a higher score. Before the first video games appeared, arcades were already a popular destination for teens and young adults to test their skills at pinball and other mechanical games. Now video games provided players with new selections and challenges to show off their talent on the arcade scene.

In 1971, Nolan Bushnell, co-founder of Atari and one of the creators of *Pong*, predicted that video games would replace pinball. He was right. Bushnell had sold four thousand *Pong* cabinets by the end of 1974. Since he had neglected to **patent** the popular game, many other companies also released copies. Bars and restaurants installed the first video game cabinets, hoping to attract adults relaxing after a hard day's work. However, the games were so popular that they soon started popping up all over the United States, and marketers began targeting kids. Grocery stores, doctor's offices, and other businesses started installing arcade games to entertain their customers and their customers' children as they browsed or

PONG IS BORN

Al Alcorn had just started a new job at Atari when his boss, Nolan Bushnell, asked him to design a Ping-Pong game. The task was meant to be a training exercise, but the game turned out to be a lot of fun to play. Bushnell decided to test the game out by setting it up at Andy Capp's Tavern in Sunnyvale, California. Soon, word had spread about the new game. *Pong* could easily make four times as much money in a week compared to a regular coin-operated machine.

waited. The number of dedicated game arcades gradually climbed as well. It helped that video games were typically cheaper to make and repair than complicated pinball tables. Also, these arcade games offered a more satisfying experience than the home gaming systems available at the time. Due to their smaller size and lower price point, home systems were much more limited in their visuals, sound effects, and speed. Plus, arcade games could easily incorporate controls beyond buttons and **joysticks**. Many arcade games included foot pedals, steering wheels, and plastic guns.

In 1978, the Japanese company Taito created what would become the most popular arcade game of the decade: *Space Invaders*. In the game, a single player attempts to protect Earth from a relentless attack of alien spaceships. Space exploration and science fiction had remained popular since the moon landing in 1969, as evidenced by the hit movie *Star Wars* (1977). *Space Invaders* drew inspiration from this film, as well as the novel *War of the Worlds* (1897) by H. G. Wells,

Opposite: *Space Invaders Part II* (1979) featured color graphics, but the game play was almost identical to the original arcade hit.

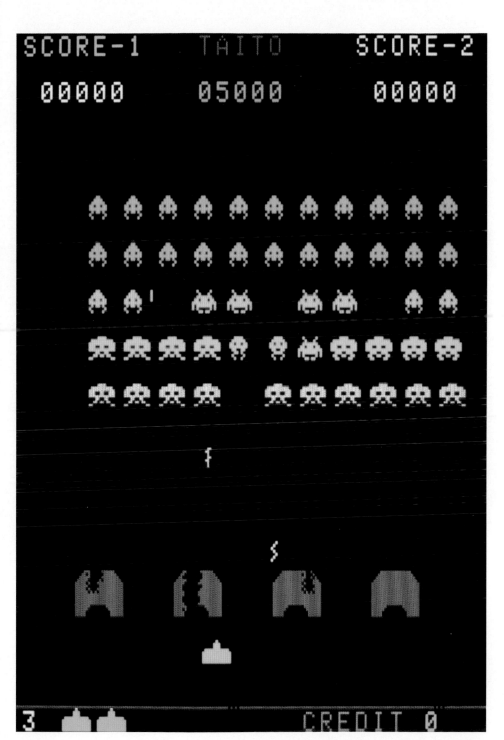

which is about aliens attacking Earth. The game was such a hit in Japan that some arcades opened with just *Space Invaders* machines. Soon, the game sparked arcade fever around the world. Atari released *Asteroids* in 1979, and a slew of popular arcade games came out in 1980, including *Berzerk*, *Pac-Man*, *Defender*, *Missile Command*, and *Rally-X*.

Arcades offered a safe haven for kids, teens, and young adults. At the time, it wasn't unusual for older children and teens to spend large amounts of time without any adult supervision. At an arcade, kids could escape from their parents and responsibilities and hang out with friends without spending a lot of money.

AT HOME WITH VIDEO GAMES

As game arcades swallowed up America's spare change, video games also started invading their living rooms. Atari commercials from the late 1970s featured the tag line: "Don't watch television tonight. Play it!" That line was directed toward people of all ages. Atari marketed its home consoles to families. The commercials showed huge groups of people—from grandparents to little kids—crowded around the television set enjoying video games. Three years after the Magnavox Odyssey made history as the first home video game system, Atari teamed up with Sears to release its Home Pong system in time for the 1975 Christmas shopping season. Customers waited in long lines to purchase the system, which only played one game: *Pong*. However, unlike the Odyssey, the more advanced Home Pong console featured sound effects and displayed the score on screen.

Over the next several years, companies produced dozens of similar consoles. These were often bulky and covered in fake wood panels. At the time, wood paneling was a fashionable choice for the sides of automobiles, interior walls, and

Jerry Lawson holds the Fairchild Channel F, the first video game console system to use cartridge technology.

appliances. Video game consoles simply followed the trend. Each console typically came with a handful of games, including *Pong* variations, hockey, target shooting, and more. At the time, it wasn't possible to purchase additional games for a console. The games were programmed into the machine itself.

That would change in 1976 when Jerry Lawson, an engineer at the company Videosoft, invented the first console to use **cartridge** technology. As an African-American engineer and inventor, Lawson was a pioneer in an industry that remains predominantly filled with white, male employees to this day. As of 2005, only 2 percent of game developers were black.

GAMES ON THE GO

Compared to cell-phone games today, the first portable video games seem ridiculously simple. In the first handheld electronic game, *Auto Race* (1976) from Mattel, the player controls a tiny red light that represents a car. The car can move left, right, up, or down. The player has to drive the light to the top of a strip, while avoiding crashing into other red lights. A year later, Mattel released *Football* (1977), a game with the same basic graphics, but this time the red light represented a quarterback.

Lawson's invention was called the Video Entertainment System but was later renamed the Fairchild Channel F after Atari released its similarly named Video Computer System the next year. Atari's system, which later became known as the Atari 2600, wound up outselling the Channel F. The Atari 2600 was successful mainly because players already knew Atari's games from the arcades. Now they could purchase game cartridges called "videocarts" and play their favorite games at home. Bushnell said, "The games that were most successful were those that were simple to learn, but impossible to master."

The Atari 2600 remained popular through the early 1980s. Hit games included home versions of the popular arcade games *Space Invaders* (1978), *Pac-Man* (1980), *Missile Command* (1980), and *Breakout* (1976), as well as original games that launched entire **genres** of game play. For example, *Pitfall* (1982) challenged players to run and jump on platforms. *Pitfall* quickly became a best seller, and now "platformer" games have their own genre.

Pitfall was created by former Atari employees who broke off and started their own company, Activision, in 1980. Activision was the first company to focus only on making video games for another company's console. Today, this type of arrangement is common. The companies that write and develop video games are not usually the same as the ones that produce and sell consoles. River Raid (1982) was another popular early Activision title that involved flying a plane over a river while shooting ships and helicopters. This was one of the first games that placed items and enemies randomly, meaning that players could not simply memorize each level —the game was different each time it was played.

A WORLD OF ADVENTURE

Most early video games required quick reflexes and lasted only a short time—exactly the type of game an arcade owner desired. The goal was to give a player an enjoyable enough experience that he or she fed quarters into the machine, but to make that experience as brief as possible. That way, other players got a turn to spend their spare change. Early computer games didn't have such constraints. In the 1970s, as in the 1960s, most people still did not own home computers. Therefore, it didn't make sense to develop a computer game as a product to bring to market. Instead, most early computer games were either experiments or labors of love programmed and played in secret on machines owned by universities and corporations.

The programmer William Crowther created one of the most famous early computer games mostly because he wanted something he could play with his kids. He called the game Colossal Cave Adventure (1976). A caver himself, Crowther had spent many hours exploring and mapping the Mammoth Cave system in Kentucky. He also enjoyed playing Dungeons and Dragons, a physical game that came out in 1974 in which players take on the roles of characters in a fantasy story, such as elves and wizards. They roll dice to determine the outcomes of their actions. *Colossal Cave Adventure* combined cave exploration with a **role-playing game** (RPG)—without any images. Players read lines from a story on the computer screen, then typed commands, such as "go south" or "unlock," to make decisions. Many commands players might try would result in frustrating responses such as "I don't know that word," but part of the fun was experimenting and learning the language of the game.

Don Woods, an academic at the Stanford Artificial Intelligence Laboratory, reworked the game with Crowther's permission, calling it simply *Adventure*. A group at MIT then

In the Atari game *Adventure*, players could discover this "Easter egg," or game secret: a hidden room that contained the name of the game's creator! However, in 2003, a newly released version of the game removed Warren Robinett's name, replacing it with the word "TEXT?"

THE FIRST EASTER EGG

In a video game, an "Easter egg" is a secret hidden in the game. It's possible to win the game without ever discovering it. Players enjoy seeking out or stumbling across these surprises. Atari's *Adventure* (1979) was the first game to include an Easter egg. At the time, games did not credit the programmers who wrote them, so the game's programmer, Warren Robinett, hid his name in a secret room.

played this game and created *Zork* (1977), perhaps the most famous text-based computer game. While these games can't exactly be considered "video" games, because there's no video involved, they led to one of the most popular video game genres: role-playing games. Woods's and Crowther's game inspired a programmer at Atari to write *Adventure* (1979). In the game, the player controlled a yellow square that explored a maze and gathered objects. The player had to use the objects to solve puzzles while avoiding dragons. Today, games with open worlds to explore such as *Skyrim* (2011) continue the tradition started by these early adventure games.

ROLE-PLAYING IN THE CLASSROOM

Even before William Crowther created *Colossal Cave Adventure*, Don Rawitsch, a student teacher in Minnesota, worked with his computer programmer roommates to develop *Oregon Trail* (1971), the first educational video game. Rawitsch created the role-playing game to teach his history students about life on the Oregon Trail, a route that many Americans followed in the nineteenth century to settle on the West Coast. Like

You are now at the Kansas River crossing. Would you like to look around? ⚒

Date: April 7, 1848
Weather: warm
Health: good
Food: 910 pounds
Next landmark: 0 miles
Miles traveled: 102 miles

On the Apple II computer, *Oregon Trail* incorporated simple graphics. Players hunted for food, forded rivers, and battled diseases as they attempted to take a wagon across the country in this educational game.

Colossal Cave Adventure, the game relied on text commands. Rawitsch later got a job with the Minnesota Educational Computing Consortium, a company that produced educational software. The company released a new version of the game, including basic graphics, in 1978 for the Apple II, one of the first successful home computers. The game has been remade again and again over the years. It remains popular today.

Eventually, this type of teaching would be dubbed "edutainment." Educational software took off in the 1980s as computers became widespread in schools and classrooms. The companies creating these games looked to popular arcade games for inspiration, but instead of blasting aliens, a player might have to blast the correct answer to a math problem. Teachers started to realize that gaming could be an incredible tool for learning and practicing new skills. Games could hold kids' interest with sounds, visuals, and stories, while adding an element of interactivity to the learning process.

THE DECADE IN REVIEW

The golden age of the arcade video game lasted from the mid-1970s through the mid-1980s. During this time, different genres of video games began to emerge. The first were arcade-style games that required speed and precision. These action games often involved shooting enemies or racing against a clock in order to get a high score. Many arcade games saved a list of the initials of the top ten high-scoring players, and it was a mark of pride for a player to have his or her name at the top of the list. The action game genre may be subdivided into many more varieties, including sports, racing, fighting, shooters, and platform games.

Meanwhile, adventure and role-playing games got their start on computers, then spread to consoles such as the Atari 2600. To beat these games, players didn't need quick reflexes. They needed intelligence, perseverance, creativity, and time. Playing a game like *Adventure* was akin to reading a book or watching a movie, but instead of sitting back and observing, the player actively participated in the story.

By the end of the 1970s, video games were impossible to avoid. They were everywhere—from the dentist's waiting area to a family's living room.

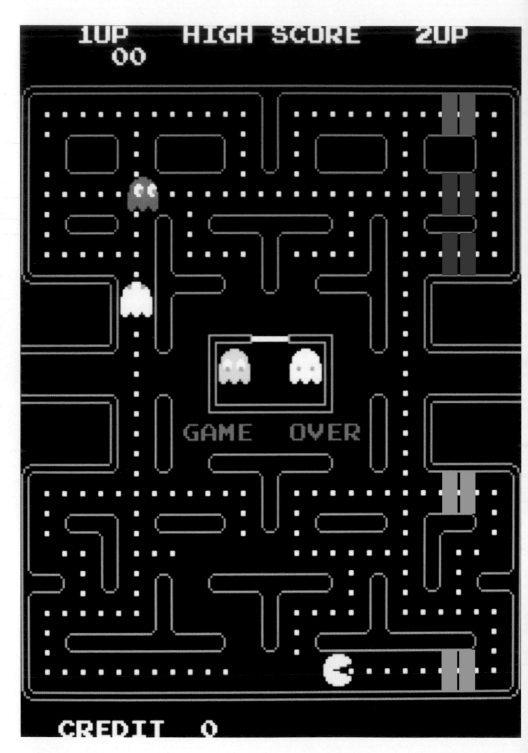

1980s:
Boom and Crash

THE YEAR 1980 ARGUABLY MARKED THE height of the golden age of video games. After *Pac-Man* came out in arcades in 1980, Pac-Mania spread across the United States. The game involved maneuvering a round, yellow character with a large mouth through a maze while avoiding ghosts. When Pac-Man chomped a power pill, though, he could temporarily chase and defeat the ghosts. For the first time, a video game character became a common sight on food packages, toys, and other products. By 1982, Pac-Man had his own cartoon on television and had inspired a pop song called "Pac-Man Fever" (1982) that reached number nine on the Billboard pop chart. Pac-Man remains a symbol of video gaming to this day.

Atari also hosted the first large-scale video game tournament in 1980, in which ten thousand players, mostly young teens, played *Space Invaders* (1978). Prizes for the highest scores included an arcade machine and a computer.

Opposite: The ghosts in *Pac-Man* were named Inky, Blinky, Pinky, and Clyde. Each had its own way of moving around the maze.

43

But the golden age couldn't last forever. In 1982, the United States entered an economic recession. Some businesses closed, and many people lost their jobs. The video game industry was no exception. A video game crash in 1983 led to the collapse of Atari, the game company that had ruled the market for almost ten years. The Japanese company Nintendo rose from the wreckage and ushered in a new era of gaming with its Nintendo Entertainment System, better known as the NES. A plumber named Mario soon became the face of this new generation of games.

The video game crash affected mostly the sale of video game consoles and cartridges, though arcades suffered as well. The number of game arcades in the United States had more than doubled between 1980 and 1982, and many of these closed down in 1983. The rising popularity of personal computers, or PCs, also contributed to the crash. Why should a family buy an expensive video game console when they could get a computer that would play games and also do so much more? In the 1980s, computer technology improved rapidly and became cheap enough for middle-class families to afford. The Commodore 64 (1982), which included a special slot to insert video game cartridges, became one of the best-selling computers in the United States. *Time* magazine named the PC "man of the year" in 1983, a sign of computers' increased popularity. This was also the first year that consumers could purchase cellular phones, though it would be years before anyone associated cell phones with gaming.

Notable historical events of the 1980s included the tragic *Challenger* shuttle explosion in 1986 that killed a crew of seven, including schoolteacher Christa McAuliffe. The AIDS epidemic also swept through the nation during the 1980s. The disease was particularly devastating in gay communities. As Americans fought to cure the disease and reduce the fear

The Commodore 64 used cartridge technology for games such as *Radar Rat Race* and *International Soccer*.

surrounding it, sexual orientation and sexuality became more mainstream topics. The decade ended with a triumph for democracy: the Berlin Wall fell in 1989, signaling the end of the Cold War.

A RICH PERSON'S DECADE

After two decades of social upheaval and idealism, conservative values made a comeback in the 1980s with the "New Right" political movement. This group emphasized patriotism and family values. They wanted the government to stop spending money on social programs that didn't seem to be working. Ronald Reagan, a former actor turned politician, won the presidency in 1980. He introduced a series of tax cuts intended to expand the economy. The idea was that if business owners had more money, they would spend it on growing their businesses. This should create more jobs or better jobs for working class people. Some referred to this as "trickle-down" economics.

Unfortunately for the working class, the "trickle-down" effect didn't work. Instead, a gap grew between the richest and poorest Americans. The number of millionaires in America almost doubled in the 1980s, but many families that had been middle class struggled to make ends meet. The government's debt also grew. While Reagan did cut some social programs, he also increased spending on the military. The United States was working to rebuild its reputation as a world power after withdrawing from Vietnam.

After the 1982 recession, the economy recovered and business boomed. For wealthy and upper-middle-class families in America, the 1980s were a time of prosperity and materialism. The young urban professional, or "yuppie," became a symbol of this decade. These were young men (and some women) born during the baby boom who now pursued high-paying jobs in large companies. They showed off their wealth by purchasing designer clothing and expensive cars.

As the rich got richer, the gaming industry benefitted. A boost in income gave many families more money to buy the computers and consoles required to play games at home. They also had more leisure time to sit and play or to visit an arcade. Other forms of entertainment also boomed during the 1980s. Cable television and MTV transformed music, and the VCR allowed families to watch movies whenever they wanted.

ATARI'S DOWNFALL

In the early 1980s, the soaring popularity of video games attracted the attention of many toy and electronics companies. A "gold rush" occurred in which companies raced to make money off of games. In the hurry to make new video game cartridges, quality often suffered. The advertisements and cover illustrations on these games often featured realistic graphics that didn't represent the content of the actual game itself. Plus, the experience of playing a game in the arcade was still better overall than playing at home.

At the time, anyone could make game cartridges for the Atari systems. Many companies made and sold cartridges without Atari's approval. Too many games were coming out, and most of them weren't any fun to play. Some companies developed games to help promote their products. Customers could collect points to mail in and exchange for a game. For example, Crest toothpaste customers could earn the game *Tooth Protectors* (1983), and Kool-Aid points could be exchanged for *Kool-Aid Man* (1983).

It wasn't just Atari's competitors making bad games. Atari released two disappointing games two years in a row. The first was a version of *Pac-Man* for the Atari 2600 that came out

THE CONTROVERSY OVER GAMES

Not everyone loved video games. As they swelled in popularity, especially among children, many parents started to worry. Some blamed video games for everything from making kids skip school to decreasing their ability to learn or concentrate. (Interestingly, recent studies have shown that games may actually improve the brain's ability to focus.) In 1982, the United States surgeon general, Dr. C. Everett Koop, said that video games could pose a health hazard. He had no scientific evidence to back up this statement but expected that research would soon support this idea.

in early 1982. The game sold well at first but then tanked as people started to actually play the game. It wasn't nearly as colorful or smooth to play as the arcade version. Then Atari released *E.T. the Extra-Terrestrial* for the 1982 Christmas shopping season. Often blamed for Atari's downfall, this game was an even bigger disappointment. The movie, directed by Steven Spielberg, came out in the summer of 1982, and Atari had just six weeks to develop the game. Again, the game sold well at first, but then customers started trying to return the cartridges. In the game, the E.T. character moved too slowly and often fell into pits. The goal was to collect phone parts before a timer counted down, but this was nearly impossible to accomplish.

Atari's competitors also produced dozens of dedicated game consoles, including the Intellivision and Intellivision II, ColecoVision, various Sears branded systems, and many more. These all provided alternatives to the Atari 2600 and the more advanced Atari 5200. The market was crowded; customers had too many consoles and too many games to choose from.

In 1983, the industry crashed, and retail stores and companies tried to get rid of unsold video game cartridges. Atari dumped many unsold cartridges, including copies of *E.T. the Extra-Terrestrial*, in a landfill in New Mexico. Some claimed that the video game fad had ended, but in fact, players simply were no longer content with low-quality games.

They wanted something better, and they got it when the Nintendo Entertainment System (NES) was released in the United States. Nintendo tightly controlled the development of games for their system in order to maintain high quality. They even installed a special chip that would prevent unauthorized games from working. Today, the companies that make games for consoles continue to go through a rigorous approval process before they can bring a new game to market.

THE MOST FAMOUS VIDEO GAME CHARACTER OF ALL

In the 1980s, very few people would consider video games an art form. It was during this time, however, that Nintendo's

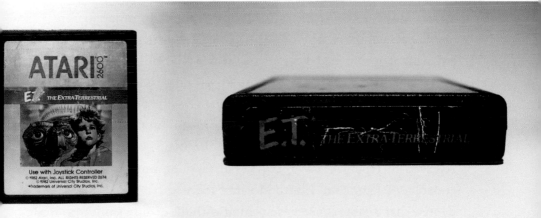

Steven Spielberg's movie *E.T. the Extra-Terrestrial* was a huge hit, but the video game was not. Some have dubbed it the worst video game of all time.

WAR Games

The Atari arcade game *Battlezone* (1980) introduced one of the first three-dimensional (3-D) worlds. In the game, the player moved through a landscape defined by green outlines and shot enemy tanks. The game caught the interest of the US military, and they requested that Atari make a version of the game that they could use for training purposes. The military would continue to show an interest in games for recruitment and training, a strategy that has proved controversial. Opponents fear that practicing fighting in a game makes it too easy for soldiers to commit violent acts in a real war.

Shigeru Miyamoto emerged as a great artist. At the time, programmers without any art or storytelling background usually designed their own games. But Miyamoto was a visual artist by training. His first big accomplishment was the arcade game *Donkey Kong* (1981). The hero of the game was a man with a moustache and overalls, dubbed Jumpman in Japan and later renamed Mario for the American audience. Mario's pet, a giant gorilla, had escaped and stolen Mario's girlfriend as revenge. The gorilla, named Donkey Kong, tossed barrels at Mario as he tried to get her back. This was one of the first arcade games to give its characters a story and motivation.

Nintendo's next big success was the NES, originally released in Japan in 1983 as the Family Computer game console, or Famicom. Nintendo had learned from Atari's demise that a game console is nothing without quality games to go with it. Miyamoto again demonstrated his brilliance as a game designer with *Super Mario Bros.* (1985). (*Mario Bros.* had been released as an arcade game in 1983 but wasn't a

The Nintendo Entertainment System rebooted the gaming industry. Cartridges were now "game paks" that users inserted into a "control deck."

huge hit.) *Super Mario Bros.* starred Mario and his brother, Luigi, as a pair of plumbers trying to rescue a princess from a creature named Bowser. The game utilized side scrolling. In most previous games, when the player reached the edge of the screen, the entire screen would reload to display the next area. Now, the player could move smoothly through the game world while the background scrolled to keep up. *Super Mario Bros.* also gradually introduced harder elements of game play. As a result, the game got more difficult as the player's skills improved. A new world wouldn't open up until the player had mastered the skills required to beat previous worlds. In addition, the game included many secrets and hidden features for dedicated gamers to unlock.

The brilliant game series Super Mario Bros. made designer Shigeru Miyamoto famous.

NINTENDO POWERS UP

Super Mario Bros. was a hit, and so was *Super Mario Bros. 2* (1988), but *Super Mario Bros. 3* (1989) cemented the series' place in video game history. The game itself was an incredible work of art. It worked with one player or two players taking turns. Players could work together or compete for points and items. The game offered myriad worlds to explore, including secret passages, mini games, and creative power-ups such as a raccoon tail that gave Mario the ability to fly.

Nintendo also came up with the perfect way to sell the game to American kids. They teamed up with Universal Pictures to feature the game in the 1989 movie *The Wizard*. In the movie, three kids make their way across the country in order to compete in a video game tournament. The game they play in the tournament is *Super Mario Bros. 3*, which hadn't yet been released in the United States. The movie was basically a giant advertisement for Nintendo and even revealed a secret in the game. Kids who were already anticipating the Mario sequel got even more psyched up. It also introduced the Power Glove, a game controller that fit over a player's hand so he or she could play a game with hand gestures. It came out in 1989, but didn't work well enough to take the place of regular controllers.

Super Mario Bros. 3 more than lived up to its dramatic debut on the big screen. The game inspired numerous copycat games, a cartoon series, and countless products. The Super Mario series proved that graphics and advanced technology don't necessarily make a game more fun. Gamers still enjoy playing the original Mario games on vintage NES systems or online emulators. Nintendo also continues to make and sell sequels, and Mario has become the best-selling game franchise

of all time. Mario is also one of the most recognized fictional characters in the world. Only Mickey Mouse can compete.

FANTASY WORLDS

The creation of Mario was enough of an accomplishment to bring Miyamoto lasting fame, but he also designed another hugely popular and influential game: *The Legend of Zelda* (1986). This game brought the open-world exploration of Atari's *Adventure* to the next level. The hero, Link, inhabited a fantastic world full of dungeons and monsters, and solved puzzles in order to progress. Players could save their progress through the game. This feature emphasizes how different this game was from high-speed, action-packed, arcade-style games. *Zelda* wasn't meant to be played in one sitting. Instead, players immersed themselves for hours in a complex fantasy world with its own mythology and history.

As the adventure game *Zelda* wowed players in both Japan and the United States, role-playing games (RPGs) split off into their own genre, including series such as Final Fantasy (begun in 1987) and Dragon Quest (started in 1986 in Japan, and originally called Dragon Warrior in the United States). In *Zelda*, the player battled enemies in real time. On the other hand, in an RPG, battles were turn-based. The player had more time to think and strategize. Also, RPG characters developed and changed throughout the game with a combination of experience, items, and special skills. The player could often customize characters, making the experience of the game unique and personal.

What all of these games had in common was a complex storyline. New Zelda and Dragon Quest games added more

Opposite: *The Wizard* may not have been a hit at the box office, but kids loved getting a sneak preview of *Super Mario Bros. 3* and the Power Glove before either product had been released.

depth to the original story, while the Final Fantasy series developed entirely new characters, settings, and stories for each new installment. These games had more in common with epic fantasy novels from the likes of J. R. R. Tolkien than they did with arcade games. They also introduced a US audience to Japanese art and mythology. An obsession with all things Japanese would become a defining feature of gaming subculture in the 1990s.

A BOYS' CLUB

By the end of the 1980s, "gamer" was emerging as an identity for many young Americans, mainly boys. Gamers flocked to video stores to rent games and eagerly anticipated each issue of *Nintendo Power*, a magazine that launched in 1988. The magazine included game tips, secrets, maps, and guides. Before *Nintendo Power* and other similar gaming magazines, this type of information had been nearly impossible to get ahold of. These magazines connected kids who loved games to each other and helped feed a growing subculture.

During Atari's reign, game advertisements had targeted entire families, and arcades drew in adults of both genders as well as teens. However, by the early 1980s, the gender balance was starting to skew toward males, perhaps due to the fact that the people developing games were predominantly men. One notable exception was Carol Shaw, a female programmer at Activision who created the popular Atari game *River Raid* (1982).

When the Japanese company Namco developed *Pac-Man* (1980), it purposefully set out to develop a game that would appeal to both women and men. *Pac-Man*'s puzzle-like game play and cartoony graphics drew in a large audience. A year later, the American company Midway developed *Ms. Pac-Man* (1981) without permission from Namco (though the

The magazine *Nintendo Power* offered its readers game maps, hints, and secrets. Before the Internet, this kind of information was difficult to find.

company later embraced the game). Advertisements for the game showed women playing, and *Electronic Games*, an early magazine devoted to gaming, ran an article titled "Women Join the Arcade Revolution." In the 1980s, the feminist movement was under attack due to the rise of conservatism in politics and popular culture. *Ms. Pac-Man*, however, welcomed women into arcades as equals to men.

That welcome did not last. By the time the movie *The Wizard* came out, the target audience for video games had narrowed. In the movie, one of the main characters was a girl, but the lead was a young, quiet boy with a hidden talent for

TOUCHDOWN!

As video games surged in popularity in the late 1970s and early 1980s, American football was also booming. In 1989, the company Electronic Arts (EA) released the first Madden football game. EA has put out a new football game almost every single year since then. Over time, the game got more and more realistic. Now, the game simulates the teams and players in the real NFL, allowing fans to feel like they are a part of the sport. EA also releases similar games for other sports, including basketball, hockey, soccer, golf, and mixed martial arts.

Each year, fans get to vote for which player should be featured on the EA Sports games' covers. *Madden NFL 11* featured quarterback Drew Brees of the New Orleans Saints.

playing video games. One of the villains was an older teen boy who owned and had mastered all the NES games in existence at the time. Boys watching the movie saw themselves in these characters. While many girls continued to enjoy games, the growing sense among game industry professionals and families alike was that video games were for boys.

HANDHELD GAMES

In 1989, Nintendo released the first Game Boy, a handheld gaming system. Earlier electronic games had been simplistic toys featuring moving lights or characters that lit up using technology similar to a digital clock. The Game Boy was different. The games were miniature computers with their own processors and memory chips. The Game Boy wasn't the first system of its kind—the Microvision came out in 1979, but didn't catch on. It didn't have any games people really wanted to play.

The Game Boy, on the other hand, came with an addictive puzzle game called *Tetris*. A Russian mathematician created the game in 1984, and despite the ongoing Cold War, the game found its way to a Western audience, who played it on computers. Nintendo thought it was perfect for the Game Boy, since it was easy to see on a tiny screen that could only display greenish graphics. They were right. The Game Boy turned the already popular puzzle game into a sensation and revolutionized handheld gaming.

THE DECADE IN REVIEW

During the 1980s, console video games briefly fell out of favor, but they returned with a vengeance. As computer technology found its way into people's homes and businesses, video games followed. They provided a visible and tangible experience of the rapid improvements occurring in hardware and software.

The computers and game systems of the 1970s simply didn't have the memory or processor speed to display any more than a grid of blocky pixels in a handful of colors. Intel developed the very first computer chip in 1971, and from then on, the amount of information one chip could hold kept increasing dramatically, allowing more and more power to be packed into smaller, cheaper machines.

In the 1980s, game systems such as the NES used faster 8-bit processors. The graphics, while still blocky, were easier to interpret and allowed for more complex game characters and worlds. However, games could display just 256 colors, and memory space was still extremely limited. By the end of the 1980s, the Japanese company Sega challenged Nintendo's dominance with one of the first 16-bit systems in 1988. Introduced as the MegaDrive in Japan, it came to be known as the Genesis in the United States. Nintendo countered with the 16-bit Super Nintendo (SNES) in 1991, and a war was on as the two companies battled for gamers' loyalty.

FIVE

1990s:
Going to Extremes

DURING THE 1990S, COMPUTER TECHNOLOGY continued to advance at breakneck speed. Computers rapidly shrunk in size, gained in power, and became more affordable. A computer that was state of the art one year would be outdated just a year or even a few months later. Video games kept pace with the advancing technology, delivering more and more realistic graphics, better sound, and more complex game mechanics. In addition, 3-D environments and online multiplayer gaming both went mainstream thanks to improved technology.

During the 1980s, even though many people enjoyed playing games on computers, most Americans saw computers primarily as tools for getting work done. By the 1990s, more and more people started using computers to have fun and express themselves. Computers became an indispensable part of modern life as governments, libraries, schools, banks, and other businesses digitized their paper records.

A new period in human history was in full swing: the information age. Scholars disagree about when, exactly, the information age started. However, it was during the 1990s that the Internet and cell phones began to erase distances between people and link together the entire world. Small networks of connected computers had been around since the 1960s, but the advent of the World Wide Web in 1989 gave people an easier way to share and access information. By the mid-1990s, the Internet had swelled to contain millions of host computers which delivered websites and e-mail to an even greater number of personal computers. By the end of the decade, people were sending more e-mails than phone calls or letters, and over one hundred million Americans owned cell phones. Investors hoping to get rich poured money into start-up Internet companies in the dot-com revolution.

Meanwhile, the audience for video games continued to skew male, and the age that game companies marketed toward rose from kids to teens to young adults. Violence in games became an increasing concern as designers piled on the blood and guts to create shocking, extreme experiences. A stereotype emerged that video games were for geeks and nerds. These were derogatory terms at the time for a smart person who enjoyed technology but lacked social skills, athletic ability, or good hygiene. Of course not all gamers fit this stereotype, but for a person who didn't fit in with society, a fantasy world could offer a welcoming escape. Thanks to the emergence of the Internet, these gamers found each other and built their own subculture.

THE CONSOLE WAR

The companies Nintendo and Sega, both based in Japan, dominated the console video game industry in the early 1990s. Arcades were still popular at this time, but more and more families owned dedicated gaming systems that now promised gaming experiences similar to the arcade. Sega ads proclaimed: "Genesis does what Nintendon't," and touted their system's technical advances. Sega developed its own cute character, Sonic the Hedgehog, in order to compete with Mario. The Genesis came to be known for its sports games, while Nintendo's specialty was adventure-style games, though many games were released for both systems. While Nintendo had marketed the NES to kids and parents as a family-friendly system, the Sega Genesis targeted older kids and teens who wanted to be cool and cutting edge. Kids were paying attention. They talked about 16-bit systems and "blast processing" on the playground.

These terms were mostly marketing hype. The number of bits a computer processor used was just one of several technological aspects that contributed to performance. It was

Players could purchase a Power Base Convertor for the Sega Genesis. This allowed them to play older Sega Master System games on the new console.

a fairly arbitrary way to measure whether one system was better than another, but thanks to Sega's marketing campaigns, gamers came to care so much about the number of bits that Nintendo's next console after the SNES was named the Nintendo 64, after its 64-bit processor. The console came out in 1996. Interestingly, many game systems today still use 64-bit processors, but the hardware has improved dramatically in other ways.

The Nintendo 64 was the last console to use cartridges, though the Game Boy and other handheld systems continued to rely on these information packs. Instead, video games followed the music and movie industries in making the switch to compact discs, better known as CDs. A CD was cheaper and easier to produce than a cartridge, and it held much more data. Sega released a CD add-on for the Genesis in 1992, but not very many companies made games for that system. Then, in 1994, Sony released the PlayStation, a 32-bit system with a CD drive. Before the system's launch, Sony worked hard to make sure that developers were interested and able to make

The first PlayStation console used CD technology.

games for the system. They even created a software library to make game development for their system easier. For example, a developer creating a game could grab a standard feature to save the game. Then, the developer wouldn't have to program that feature from scratch.

Sega had raised the target audience for video games from kids to teens. Sony continued this trend and set its sights on young men who had grown up playing video games. By the end of the decade, PlayStation was the most popular video game console.

TRAGEDIES ABROAD AND AT HOME

During the 1990s, the levels of sex and violence in all forms of media increased. It became more common for mainstream music and music videos, movies, television shows, and video games to feature graphic content. Everyone wanted to be "edgy." The news was no exception as TV stations broadcast tragic historical events.

The Cold War had ended with the fall of the Berlin Wall in 1989. Then, in 1991, the United States entered the Persian Gulf War. Though this conflict lasted less than a year, Americans would become involved in a second phase of the war in 2003. The TV news covered these wars with brutal detail. In 1992, Democrat Bill Clinton was elected to his first of two terms as president. That same year, the people of Los Angeles rioted after a bystander filmed white police officers beating a black man after a car chase. In 1994, the trial of O. J. Simpson, a famous football player accused of murdering his wife and her friend, also sparked discussions about race. Simpson, who was acquitted after a highly televised trial, was black, while the victims and lead detective were white. Despite the progress made by the civil rights movement, racial tensions remained high in many cities.

Other acts of violence also stunned the country, including the Oklahoma City bombing in 1995 and the capture that same year of the Unabomber, a man who had been sending bombs in the mail. Both of these terrorists were white male Americans. Finally, in 1999, another senseless and horrific act occurred: two teen boys walked into their high school cafeteria and started shooting. They killed thirteen people, mostly other students, and wounded several dozen in what came to be known as the Columbine High School massacre. In the period of grieving that followed, many pointed their fingers at one of the shooters' favorite pastimes: video games. They questioned whether violent games may have factored into the teens' decision to commit murder.

WARNING SIGNS

Several years before the Columbine shooting, the level of brutality in *Mortal Kombat* (1992), a popular arcade video game, sparked controversy. The game pitted two fighters against each other, and each match ended with the opportunity to finish the opponent off with a move called a fatality. For example, the winner might rip the loser's heart or spine from his or her body. Nintendo, in keeping with its family-friendly image, chose to censor its version of *Mortal Kombat* for the SNES. They took out the blood and fatalities. Sega kept them in, however, and the uncensored game sold much better.

At the time, game companies were just starting to target older audiences, but games were still sold in toy stores and didn't have a consistent ratings system that might warn parents and kids about such violent content. Sega had placed labels on *Mortal Kombat* indicating that it was intended for a mature audience of the age of thirteen and older, but this solution wasn't good enough for some parents and lawmakers. On December 9, 1993, the US Senate held a hearing about

Scorpion battles Reptile in *Mortal Kombat 2*. This sequel introduced new characters and new, more gruesome fatality moves.

inappropriate content in video games. They scrutinized *Mortal Kombat* and also *Night Trap* (1992), a game that included cut scenes showing attacks on scantily clad women. The hearing led to the establishment of the Entertainment Software Rating Board (ESRB) in 1994.

VIDEO GAME RATINGS

eC: Early childhood. These games are for very young children.

E: Everyone. May contain some cartoon or mild violence.

E10+: For ages ten and up. May contain more cartoon or mild violence.

T: Teens ages thirteen and up. May contain violence and some blood, strong language, or suggestive themes.

M: Mature players ages seventeen and up. May contain intense violence, blood and gore, or sexual content.

AO: Adults only

THE *DOOM* EFFECT

By complete coincidence, one day after the hearing, id Software released *Doom* (1993). One of the best and most influential games of the decade, *Doom* popularized the first-person shooter genre. In this style of game, there is no character on the screen to control—just a hand holding a weapon, typically a gun. This makes the player feel as if he or she is in the game world, wielding a weapon. In *Doom*, the player became a soldier fighting his or her way through a maze full of terrifying monsters. The game was released as shareware on the PC, meaning that people were free to copy and share the first third of the game with friends. (They had to pay to purchase the rest). It spread quickly across the country.

Doom helped introduce players to 3-D graphics. Technically, the game was still two-dimensional (2-D); it used tricks of perspective to create the illusion of depth. However, *Doom*'s sequel, *Quake* (1996), used an actual 3-D environment and characters. Arcade games such as *I, Robot* (1983) and

The creators of the game *Doom* made the source code freely available. This means that people can supply their own art, sound, and level designs. The Freedoom project collects this content in order to create a completely free game.

Virtua Racing (1992) were the first to experiment with 3-D graphics. PlayStation and other game consoles introduced 3-D games in the 1990s as well. Displaying 3-D graphics required more computing power than had previously been available. In 2-D games such as *Super Mario Bros.*, only one flat side of a character, called a sprite, could be viewed at a time. In a 3-D game, the camera could pan smoothly all around a character or all around the environment.

69

Doom was also one of the first popular games to offer an online multiplayer mode. Playing together over the Internet wasn't completely new. In 1980, a pair of students at Essex University in England built a game they called *MUD*, for *Multi-User Dungeon*. They took their inspiration from text adventure games but made it possible for anyone to connect to the game over a computer network. This type of gaming would eventually lead to the massive virtual universes found in games such as *World of Warcraft* (2001).

In *Doom*'s multiplayer mode, up to four players (and later up to sixteen), each on their own computers, could connect through the Internet and play together. These players fought each other. Each time a player killed an opponent, that player would get a point. Then, the opponent would come back to life, or respawn, to continue fighting. Finally, *Doom* broke new ground by offering players a level editor and access to alter the sound and visual effects in the game. Players could build their own versions of the game, and millions did. A community emerged of people creating, sharing, and playing "mods" (or modified versions) of *Doom*.

A DANGER TO SOCIETY?

Two of the many players who created a mod of *Doom* happened to be the Columbine shooters. In 2007, a psychiatrist noted that the boys had carried out the attack after their parents had taken away their access to computers. He theorized that games such as *Doom* allowed the boys to act out their aggressive impulses but that they were unable to separate fantasy violence from real-world violence. Many studies have linked violence in the media to increased aggressive thoughts or feelings in children, but there is no conclusive evidence to show that playing a violent game can actually transform a normal person into a killer. In 2001, the surgeon general of the United States reported that media was not necessarily a cause of violence. Instead, a person who already has violent tendencies may be more drawn to this type of game. For some people, playing a violent video game could offer a safe way to vent anger. In addition, some experts have shown that the release of a new video game actually coincides with fewer violent crimes. The theory is the people who would be out committing crimes stay home to play the game instead.

Video games are the newest form of entertainment to come under public scrutiny. Society has a long track record of blaming new forms of media for corrupting or harming children. Radio, movies, and television have also been criticized in the past for taking up too much of kids' time and for feeding them unsavory thoughts and ideas. In the end, the conclusion seems to be that it is not the form of entertainment that matters, but the content of the media and the psychological condition of the child watching, listening, or playing. Parents and guardians are responsible for making sure that children play games that are age appropriate.

SEX AND VIOLENCE

Video game controversies continued to capture public attention with the release of the console games *Tomb Raider* (1996) and *Grand Theft Auto* (1997). *Grand Theft Auto* was the first game in what would become one of the best-selling series of games ever, but the series attracted negative attention because the games cast players in the role of criminals that could steal cars, run over pedestrians, and wreak havoc, all while avoiding the police.

The spotlight on *Tomb Raider*, meanwhile, involved the game's hero: Lara Croft. She was a sexy female adventurer reminiscent of Indiana Jones, the lead in a popular movie series that came out in the 1980s. At the time, PlayStation's

target audience was older teen boys and young adult men. A PlayStation commercial from 1998 showed a young man in a movie theater with his girlfriend. PlayStation characters, including Lara Croft, surrounded him and asked him whether he'd like to stay there watching a "chick flick" with his nagging girlfriend, or go home and shoot a bazooka? As a sex symbol, Lara Croft helped draw in young men. Many feminists criticized this as an example of how women are objectified for men's benefit. However, others have reclaimed Lara Croft as one of gaming's first important female heroes. A 2013 sequel to the original *Tomb Raider* focused on developing Lara's character and making her inner struggles more important than her looks.

GAMES AND MOVIES

Popular stories and characters leave an impression on popular culture and spur spin-offs. Those stories may originate in a movie, book, or even a video game. In the 1980s and early 1990s, it was more common to see video game adaptations of movies. Early examples include *E.T. the Extra-Terrestrial* (1982), *Aladdin* (1992), and countless games based on *Star Wars*. Starting in the 1990s, some video games became popular enough to lead to movie adaptations. The films *Mortal Kombat* (1995) and *Lara Croft: Tomb Raider* (2001) both attracted large audiences. Now, game previews commonly play alongside film previews in theaters.

Opposite: Angelina Jolie starred in the 2001 movie *Lara Croft: Tomb Raider*.

WOMEN IN GAMES

Whether Lara Croft was a sex symbol or a role model, the fact remains that in the 1990s, many games appealed more to boys than girls. Game companies' market research indicated that males were much more likely to play games, so they made games they thought males would enjoy and created advertising targeted toward males. This drew in more boys and pushed away many girls.

However, one computer game proved an exception to this rule: *Myst* (1993). The player explored a beautiful, mysterious island, solving puzzles in an attempt to escape. The game gradually revealed a narrative, making the experience of playing the game somewhat similar to reading a novel. There were no

In *Myst*, players solved puzzles in order to advance through the game.

enemies to fight, and no guidance about what to do first or where to go next. The game reached a wide audience including women and men, senior citizens and teens, and experienced gamers and people who had never played video games before. It became one of the best-selling computer games of all time.

GAMES AS ART

By the late 1990s, games began to look more like movies. They employed cut scenes, voice-overs, soundtracks, and scrolling credits. The game *Final Fantasy VII* (1997) was one of the first to use cut scenes throughout the game to tell a story and develop characters. *Metal Gear Solid* (1998) also helped introduce cinematic effects and established a new genre: the stealth game. For much of the game, the player took on the role of a soldier attempting to infiltrate enemy bases. The goal was to sneak past guards without being seen. While the player could kill enemies, this approach often made the game more difficult. The first Metal Gear game came out in 1987, and the series continued through 2015. Designed by Hideo Kojima, these games were masterpieces of ingenuity and design. Despite the fact that the games are about soldiers, they also convey an antiwar message.

Kojima played with the concept of the "fourth wall." This idea comes from the theater, where three walls enclose the stage to the sides and in the back. The fourth wall is the invisible one between the play and the audience. In a game, the fourth wall is what separates the virtual world from reality. At one point in *Metal Gear Solid*, the player had to enter a certain frequency. This number did not exist within the game—the player had to find it on the game's physical CD case. Later, in order to beat a boss, the player had to unplug the game controller and plug it into the other slot. Kojima was exploring the boundaries of the video game art form.

GAMER CULTURE

Games offered an escape from reality and drew in many of society's misfits. These geeks banded together with the mutual feeling that the rest of society misunderstood them and their favorite games. The geekiest games of all were fantasy adventures, particularly RPGs. Many RPGs came from Japan, and a fan of these games would often also follow other aspects of Japanese culture, including comic books, movies, and clothing. The biggest Japanese influence of all came from anime, a term for a cartoony style of animation. Anime boomed in popularity in the United States in the 1990s, partially thanks to a bunch of cute little monsters called Pokémon.

Pokémon started out in Japan as a pair of games for the handheld Game Boy system called *Pocket Monsters Red* and *Green* (1996). The games involved collecting different types of anime-style monsters, training them, and then fighting battles with them. Trading cards inspired by the games came

McDonald's restaurants have included Pokémon toys and cards in kids' meals.

76

out in Japan that same year. In 1998 and 1999, the games and cards arrived in the United States, kicking off a Pokémon craze among grade-school kids. At that time in the United States, the trading card game *Magic: The Gathering* was hugely popular, especially among gamers and geeks. The Pokémon card game offered a similar style of play but with simpler rules that made it easier for kids to learn. Both games involved purchasing packs of random cards in the hopes of finding rare, powerful cards. Pokémon cards surged in popularity, leading many schools to ban them. This success led to a Pokémon cartoon, movie, and of course more video games. The series remains popular today.

DECADE IN REVIEW

During the 1990s, game technology improved dramatically, game genres continued to diversify, and video games emerged as an art form. First-person shooters and stealth games resonated with a video game audience composed mainly of male teens and young adults. *Resident Evil* (1996) was one of the first survival horror games. These games employed terrifying settings and storylines. The player had to carefully manage resources in order to survive. *Gran Turismo* (1997) revolutionized racing games, offering an experience so realistic it was almost a simulation of driving a real car.

SimCity (1989), a game in which players built up and managed a city, demonstrated that games didn't need enemies or even a way to win. This game gave players the tools to build and manage a city. They would construct buildings and roads, collect taxes, and deal with natural disasters that could set back development. The game's success led the developer to release a series of sequels and spin-off titles over the next few decades, from *SimAnt* (1991) to *SimFarm* (1993). Strategy games also took a step forward with the release of *Civilization* (1991), a game that challenged players to guide a single civilization from the stone age through the space age.

Outside of the gamer subculture, other games also had a cultural impact. In the 1990s, the Windows operating system revolutionized the world of personal computing. Every single Windows system came with the card game *Solitaire* included for free. People around the world snuck in games of *Solitaire* while they were supposed to be working. In fact, people have played this simple card game more times than they've used any other Windows program, such as Excel, Word, or Internet Explorer.

Windows *Solitaire* and *Tetris* on the Game Boy both demonstrate the appeal of casual gaming and the importance of games as a way for people to learn about and engage with new technology. By the late 1990s and early 2000s, the cell phone began to morph from a portable telephone into a miniature computer, complete with e-mail, an Internet browser, a camera, and games. Once a symbol of the very wealthy, cell phones quickly became an indispensable part of modern life and made video games accessible any time, anywhere.

2000s:
The Rise of the Geek

BY THE EARLY 2000S, GAMERS HAD CEMENTED their reputation as socially awkward teen boys or young men still living in their parents' basements, but this image was about to change. As laptops, tablets, cell phones, search engines, and social media transformed how people communicated, games went mainstream. Escaping into fantasy worlds became more socially acceptable as well, as demonstrated by the runaway popularity of the Harry Potter books (the first came out in 1997) and the Lord of the Rings movies (beginning in 2001). However, the acceptance of both geeks and their games came about mainly thanks to the continued rise and spread of computer technology. Wherever computers went, games followed. Soon, enjoying technology wasn't unusual or antisocial; it was essential.

Thanks to the rise of the Internet, mobile devices, and other technology, gaming was no longer a solitary or even a stationary pursuit. Strangers played together online. New systems to track physical movement got players off the couch and moving. Mobile devices led to the development of simple, casual games. Independent games took off with the help of distributors such as the Steam store on the PC and app stores for mobile devices. Meanwhile, traditional video games played on consoles or on computers became increasingly realistic, cinematic, and culturally important.

By the 2010s, gamers themselves were perhaps the most surprised to learn that the geeks had risen, and gaming was suddenly cool.

TERROR STRIKES

The new millennium opened with a horrific tragedy. On September 11, 2001, terrorists from an Islamic extremist group called al-Qaeda took over control of four passenger jets. They crashed two of them into the World Trade Center towers in New York City and a third into the Pentagon. The fourth was headed for the White House, but passengers managed to overtake the hijackers and crash the plane before it reached its target. In the wake of the attack, American patriotism surged and President George W. Bush launched a war against terror. This included an attack on Afghanistan, where al-Qaeda leaders were believed to be hiding. A few years later, the United States invaded Iraq in search of weapons of mass destruction that supposedly threatened the country. When Americans later found out that these weapons had never existed, many were angry, yet the United States remained embroiled in the Iraq War until 2011. That same year, American forces tracked down and killed Osama bin Laden, the mastermind behind the 9/11 attack.

In 2005, tragedy struck in the form of a hurricane. Hurricane Katrina triggered massive flooding in New Orleans and nearby areas, leaving over a thousand people dead and many more homeless. African Americans living in poverty were among the hardest hit by the storm. Their plight brought attention to both minorities and poor people in America. In a victory for civil rights, Americans elected the first black president in 2008: Barack Obama.

PROTESTING WALL STREET

Obama's election happened to coincide with a devastating economic recession. After a stock market crash at the end of 2008, the unemployment rate soared and many Americans lost their homes. Major banks teetered on the verge of collapse, and the government wound up supplying them with funding to keep them from failing. All of this led to a feeling of outrage among working Americans, and they responded with the Occupy Wall Street movement in 2011. This series of protests aimed to put an end to corruption among banks and corporations. The protestors argued that the wealthiest Americans, whom they dubbed the "one percent," were controlling the country and taking advantage of everyone else, the "ninety-nine percent." These protestors used new means of communication, including the social networking sites Facebook and Twitter, to express their dissatisfaction.

VIRTUAL WARFARE

As young men donned uniforms and traveled overseas to fight real battles in Iraq, many who stayed home fought virtual battles. Video games offered fighting experiences with increasingly realistic visuals, sound, and movements. The computer giant Microsoft launched its first game console, the Xbox, in 2001. By this time, console makers knew very well that a new console couldn't succeed without really great games to play on it. Xbox launched alongside a selection of games exclusively available on the new system. One of those games was *Halo: Combat Evolved* (2001). This first-person shooter planted the player in the midst of a futuristic war zone. The game's enemies were programmed with basic

Call of Duty: Modern Warfare 2 came out in 2009. The game takes place primarily in Afghanistan, continuing the story begun in *Modern Warfare*.

artificial intelligence. Sometimes, they seemed to outsmart the player.

Yet another first-person shooter, *Call of Duty* (2003), sent players back to World War II to take on the role of soldiers. Throughout the game, artificially intelligent allies fought on the human player's side. The goal of the game was to simulate the actual experience of being on a battlefield. For example, when an explosion went off near the player, the game would slow down, the graphics would blur, and a ringing sound would play. In 2007, the sequel *Call of Duty: Modern Warfare* came out. This time, instead of a historical battlefield, players fought in the Middle East. Although the events in the game were fiction, the setting and equipment mirrored the very real conflict taking place at the same time in Iraq.

AMERICA'S ARMY

The US military had been following video games since the very beginning. In the 1990s, the Marine Corps produced a modified version of *Doom II* to function as a training exercise. Then, in 2002, the US Army funded and released the game *America's Army*. The first-person shooter was available free online or at army recruitment offices. The game matched

Army recruiters watch for young adults who might be interested in joining the military. The free game *America's Army* was created as a recruitment tool.

other similar games on the market in quality, but it wasn't all for fun. It functioned as a recruiting tool, allowing players to try out different roles within the army. The goal was to get kids interested in enlistment.

Critics started to worry that these kinds of games were glorifying combat while deadening kids to the reality of war. When a player dies in a video game, he or she can usually come right back to life. Injuries don't actually hurt, and the enemies aren't real people. Meanwhile, real combat became more game-like as soldiers began controlling robotic drones to carry out strikes. Soldiers in the field, however, have said that their job is nothing like a video game and they can easily separate the fantasy from reality.

BIG AND EXPENSIVE

In the early days of video games, a single programmer or a small team of two or three people regularly produced games. By the 2000s, large game-development companies were hiring huge teams of programmers, artists, and designers and spending millions of dollars to make just one game. These games typically promised players a cinematic experience, expansive world, and long hours of game play.

Big game publishers often chose to develop content that had already proved popular. This mirrored the trend in cinema of producing sequels to popular movies. The hope was that everyone who enjoyed the original content would pay for the sequel, too. The Call of Duty series now includes over twenty games and game expansions. The action game *Assassin's Creed* (2007) proved so popular that the company decided to release a new title every year. The game company EA puts out a new sports title for multiple major sports every year, and fans have to buy the new game in order to stay up to date with the rosters of players.

When the consoles Xbox 360 (2005) and PlayStation 3 (2006) launched, the standard price of a new video game rose from $49.99 to $59.99. People who could afford it purchased these games new at retail stores such as GameStop. When they were finished playing, they could sell the game back to the store, and others could buy the used game for a discounted price. However, by the end of the decade, it didn't make much as sense to buy a video game on a physical disc. Instead, customers could download video games and other software directly from an online store. As the popularity of e-readers such as the Kindle rose and started to replace paper books, video games also began to shed their physical packages.

PLAYING TOGETHER

The advent of the Internet also made new forms of multiplayer gaming possible. *Halo, Call of Duty*, and other similar first-person shooter games followed *Doom's* lead and offered online multiplayer battles where players could test their skills against each other. *Counter-Strike* (1999) was a first-person shooting game that could only be played over a network, against other human players. However, all of these multiplayer games existed only for the time it took to play them. When a new battle started, an environment would generate. After the battle, the environment went away. There was no reason for a game to exist without anyone playing it. Or was there?

VAST WORLDS

In the late 1990s, a new type of game genre emerged: **massively multiplayer online**, or MMO. Players experienced events at the same time, in the same world. Things continued to happen in the world even when the player left. Players could band together to complete quests, or trade items with each other. Events could happen in the world that affected all players. Games that pioneered the MMO model included *Ultima Online* (1997) and *EverQuest* (1999), but it was *World of Warcraft* (2001) that became a runaway success. Instead of a player-versus-player model, these games pitted players against the environment. Human players had to work together to complete quests and defeat computer-controlled enemies and bosses. The heart of the game was in creating and improving a character. Each completed quest increased a character's skills, experience, and resources. The higher a character's level, the more attention and respect that player would earn from others in the gaming universe.

Nicknamed *WoW* by its players, *World of Warcraft* became popular as social media sites such as Facebook (founded in 2004) were taking off. On social media, people created profiles, connected with friends, and regularly checked in for status updates. Similar networking happened (and still happens)

The *Mists of Pandaria* expansion for *World of Warcraft* came out in 2012. It introduced a new race of panda monks.

in *WoW*. Players band together into guilds and coordinate raids in which they attempt to beat a challenge in the game. In order to keep the game running, the game company, Blizzard Entertainment, charges players a monthly subscription fee. The company also continually releases new content and upgrades for the game. As a result, *World of Warcraft* has made over eight billion dollars. In addition, some people make real money selling gold and items in the game. In many ways, *WoW* is much more than a game. It is a way of life with its own economy, social conventions, and evolving history and culture.

FUN FOR ALL

Especially during the early part of the 2000s, playing *WoW* was synonymous with the label "geek," and that label brought to mind socially awkward teen boys. This stereotype may not have been entirely deserved (many girls enjoyed *WoW*), but it had some basis in reality. As of 2004, one-third of video game players were under eighteen, and almost two-thirds were male, but that was about to change. By 2010, only about 25 percent of players were under eighteen, and the gender balance was starting to equal out as well. As of 2014, women were actually slightly more likely than men to play video games.

A combination of new types of games and new technologies triggered this shift in the audience. *The Sims*, a game by the creators of *SimCity*, came out in 2000 and quickly became a best seller, especially among women. In the game, players created virtual characters, built and furnished their homes, and controlled their daily lives. The characters would wander around and make some decisions on their own, but needed direction to eat, sleep, go to work, or use the bathroom. The game's success paved the way for new types of games that appealed to a wider audience.

Game Awards

Games have only recently been accepted as a legitimate art form with their own competitions and awards. While there is no equivalent of a single Academy Awards event for video games, many different organizations bestow yearly awards for everything from Best Graphics and Best Original Score to Character of the Year. Museums have also begun to pay attention to video games. In 2012, the Smithsonian held an exhibition called *The Art of Video Games*.

SAME-SEX RELATIONSHIPS

The year 2000 also happened to be the year that Vermont made civil unions legal for same-sex couples. *The Sims* mirrored this milestone by allowing same-sex romantic relationships between characters. At a live presentation of the game at the E3 expo in 1999, two female characters kissed each other. The game designers hadn't planned for this to happen and they weren't trying to make a statement. They simply wanted to make the game as lifelike as possible. The gay rights movement went on to win support—and face opposition—across the country. State after state passed laws either legalizing or banning same-sex marriage. Finally, the Supreme Court put an end to the debate in 2015 by making same-sex marriages legal across the country.

GAMES GET MOVING

New technologies also helped bring games into the mainstream. While most of the video game industry focused on making game systems more powerful and more realistic, Nintendo took a different approach. While their new system was in development in the early 2000s, they called it the "Revolution."

They wanted to make playing games easy and appealing to whole families. To do this, they built a smaller, cheaper system with simple cartoon graphics. The real revolution, though, was in the technology behind the controller. It used motion sensors to detect the player swinging his or her arm.

Nintendo's new system came out in 2006 with the name "Wii." It took the world by storm. Across the United States and abroad, people stood up and moved around their living rooms, swinging controllers to whack a virtual baseball or tennis ball. While traditional video games tended to have complicated controls or storylines, anyone could pick up a Wii Remote and play. Even seniors at retirement communities got in on the fun. By 2010, sales of the Wii had passed those of the NES back in the 1980s.

High-school students play Wii boxing at a local teen center.

THE OBESITY EPIDEMIC

Wii Sports (2006) and *Wii Fit* (2007), an exercise program, also addressed a rising social concern in America: obesity. From the 1990s through the 2000s, the percentage of overweight Americans increased. Kids and adults were eating more and exercising less. Experts theorized that people were spending too much time sitting in front of screens, including the TV, the computer, and video games. First Lady Michelle Obama started the "Let's Move!" campaign in 2010 with the goal of raising healthier children in America.

While video games are certainly no stand-in for regular exercise, some types of games do get kids and adults moving. The term "exergaming" refers to any media that combines games with exercise. Games like this had existed since the 1980s. The Atari Joyboard, released in 1982, required players to balance on a board and lean to control the game. However, this type of play didn't become popular until the 2000s. Playing *Wii Sports* expended about as much energy as taking a walk. *Dance Dance Revolution* (1998) and other dancing games also became very popular during the 2000s. In this game and others like it, players stepped, jumped, and spun on a mat that was connected to the game system. The game *Rock Band* (2007) also got people off the couch and jamming with controllers shaped like instruments. Scientific studies have shown that active video games are a good form of exercise. However, people have to actually play the games regularly to get the benefit.

MOBILE GAMES

The Wii was an important milestone in the history of video games, but another technology completely transformed world culture in the 2000s: the cell phone. No aspect of life was

eSPORTS

Some lucky people play games competitively for a living. Cyber athletes participate in eSports, short for electronic sports. Gaming leagues and competitions have been around since the first Atari game tournament in the 1980s. Major League Gaming, established in 2002, sought to organize and support professional gaming in much the same way that the NFL supports football. The game *League of Legends* (2009), an online battle arena that pits two teams against each other, has become the most popular eSport in America.

untouched by the fact that most people had a computer at their fingertips all day long, everywhere they went. In the 1990s and early 2000s, some cell phones offered simple puzzle games such as *Tetris* or *Snake* (1997), but mobile gaming didn't take off until Apple opened its App Store in 2008. The iPhone (2007) was one of the first products to merge a mobile phone with music, Internet access, a camera, and more. Apple gave developers access to produce **applications**, called "apps," for the iPhone. Video games quickly became the largest and most popular category in the app store, competing only with social media.

Like *Solitaire* on the PC, games on smartphones became a popular distraction for people of all ages and both genders. They played these games while standing in line, riding on the subway, or waiting for an appointment. As a result, the most successful games offered quick bouts of play. After its initial launch as a PC game in 2001, the puzzle game *Bejeweled* moved to the iPhone and found a larger audience than ever before. The game is simple: match three or more of the same gem. Many sequels and copycat games, including *Candy Crush Saga* (2011) have built off of this basic concept. *Angry Birds* (2009) was another early hit. The game involved using a catapult to aim and fire birds at a group of pigs. Today, the Angry Bird characters are almost as iconic as Pac-Man or Mario, with their own T-shirts, toys, and other products.

The Angry Birds series includes games with holiday, space, and Star Wars themes.

THE SOCIAL SCENE

As mobile games drained smartphone batteries, social games invaded Facebook. The social network grew to include a staggering five hundred million users by 2011—that's one out of every thirteen people on Earth. In 2009, Zynga released the game *FarmVille* (which basically copied an earlier game, *Farm Town*). Within a few months, millions of Facebook users were growing crops and raising animals on virtual farms. The twist was that players could send gifts to their Facebook friends or invite them to visit their farms. Zynga followed up this success with the mobile game *Words with Friends* (2009). Players invited their Facebook friends or phone contacts to play a turn-based Scrabble-style crossword game.

GAMING FOR FREE

FarmVille and *Words with Friends* were both free to download and play. This trend in mobile and social gaming became increasingly widespread in the late 2000s. Many games for the iPhone or other smartphones were offered as free downloads. The developer made money in one of two ways. Either they sold ad space in the game or they tempted players to purchase extra content or bonuses within the game. Some free-to-play games gave players ways to unlock this content for free, but they had to wait a long time, slowly building up resources. For a small fee, they could advance more quickly. Other games started offering both a free version with ads and a paid version without any interruptions. People got used to trying out games and other apps before they had to commit to making a purchase.

STEAM AND THE RISE OF THE INDIE GAME

The small size of a smartphone lowered people's expectations for the look and feel of video games. Basic graphics and simple game play could succeed. Game designers didn't need a huge team or millions of dollars to produce a competitive product. App stores and other online marketplaces also gave small developers an easy way to reach a huge audience. Also, the software required to create games became cheaper throughout the 2000s. Some simple game-making programs were even available for free. All of these factors led to a rise in the number of independent game developers making what came to be known as "indie" games.

In 2003, the game developer Valve set up an online store called Steam. The company wanted a way to distribute its games directly to players, and also a way to easily provide updates or fixes to games players already owned. In addition, the company was looking for a way to combat game piracy. This problem has plagued all kinds of computer software and media. Pirates are people who copy and distribute software or media content without permission from the original creators.

In 2004, Valve released *Half-Life 2*, a highly anticipated sequel to *Half-Life* (1998). These computer games were cinematic, first-person shooters in which the player fought mutant monsters in a futuristic world. Gamers could buy *Half-Life 2* as a download from the Steam store or from a retail store, but no matter how they purchased it, they had to install Steam in order to verify their copy and play the game. Valve soon opened up the Steam store to other computer game developers. In 2013, over six hundred new games debuted on Steam and seventy-five million people had Steam accounts.

Thanks to Steam and various app stores, independent game developers could now distribute games instantly to a huge audience without needing to create a physical disc or case or get shelf space in a bricks-and-mortar store.

KICKSTARTER

The indie game movement led to a creative renaissance in video games. Without the restrictions of a game publisher or a console maker, developers could produce weird, quirky games. Some developers turned to a new Internet trend: crowdfunding. The website Kickstarter launched in 2009. People could post a project idea on the site and ask for money to fund its creation. People who "backed" the project would only pay if the project earned enough money, and then they would eventually receive the product when it was completed. Game developers could test their game ideas on an audience before even building it, and gamers could pay for a game before it had even been made.

MINECRAFT

The computer game *Minecraft* (2009) proved that even today, simple games can become huge hits. One person, best known by his nickname "Notch," created *Minecraft*. In the game, players explored a randomly generated environment, gathered resources, and used those resources to build objects. It became the most successful indie game ever, mainly thanks to the fact that players could work together and could also modify the game. Kids especially loved to build things in the game—it was almost like playing with virtual Lego bricks. The blocky graphics of the game even looked sort of like Legos.

Minecraft started out as a computer game, but now kids can play on mobile devices, too.

LOOKING FORWARD

In the 2010s, mobile games continued to spread. As the speed, memory, and computing power of mobile devices increased, these games became more cinematic and realistic than had been possible in the 2000s. Despite the fact that most mobile games are either free to download or cost less than five dollars, the mobile gaming industry could bring in more money than console games before the end of the decade.

In mainstream culture, popular video games are now as omnipresent as popular movies, books, or TV shows. Some people even enjoy watching others play games. The website Twitch (2011) streams live videos of people playing games. This trend follows the popularity of YouTube videos and the rise of YouTube stars. Some of the people on Twitch are stars as well. They've made careers playing games and providing commentary for their fans.

In 2012, Nintendo launched the Wii U, and then in 2013, the new PlayStation 4 and Xbox One consoles came out. These systems do much more than just play video games. By the 2010s, almost every device, whether it is a cell phone, a tablet, or a video game console, serves multiple purposes. The PlayStation 4 also plays high quality blu-ray movies, and the Xbox One serves as a complete entertainment center that users can control with their voices or gestures. Users can also download apps for either system. The PlayStation Vita, a handheld system, allows players to continue playing their favorite console games while on the go. The Vita streams the game from the player's PlayStation 4 system.

Video games have also started to employ effects that make a game seem to lift off from the screen into three dimensions. Nintendo released the 3-DS handheld game system in 2010. Players can turn the visual effect on or off. John Carmack, the programmer who created the pioneering games *Doom* and *Quake*, is working on technology that gives players an immersive virtual reality experience. They don a helmet and are able to literally walk around within a game world. His company released a virtual reality helmet called the Oculus Rift in 2016.

As games draw people deeper into virtual worlds, these virtual worlds also have the power to change our reality. In 2008, eight thousand people played the game *Superstruct*, in which they came up with creative ideas intended to improve the actual future of health, food, security, and more. In 2011, the online game *FoldIt* challenged people all over the world to fold proteins, only this wasn't just a game—protein folding was a difficult scientific problem that computers still couldn't master. The solutions people came up with gave chemists important information that they could use to invent new medicines or treatments for diseases. In the future, video games will continue to provide immersive entertainment while also changing the world we live in.

A young gamer tries out the Oculus Rift virtual reality headset at the E3 Entertainment Expo in 2013.

Notes

CHAPTER ONE

p. 11, "very ... chess." Turing, Alan M. "Proposed Electronic Calculator." Executive Committee of the National Physical Laboratory, February 1946, http://www.alanturing.net/ace/index.html#p01-016.

p. 15–16, "It ... society." Lambert, Bruce. "Brookhaven Honors a Pioneer Video Game," *New York Times*, November 7, 2008, http://www.nytimes.com/2008/11/09/nyregion/long-island/09videoli.html?pagewanted=print&_r=0.

CHAPTER TWO

p. 18, "That's ... mankind." "July 20, 1969: One Giant Leap For Mankind," NASA, July 14, 2014, http://www.nasa.gov/mission_pages/apollo/apollo11.html.

p. 19, "the ... decade." Batchelor, Bob, ed. *American Pop: Popular Culture Decade by Decade, 1960–1989.* Westport, CT: Greenwood Press, 2009.

CHAPTER THREE

p. 31, "a ... movie." "'Death Race' Video Game Outrages U.S. Safety Council." The Register-Guard, December 26, 1976, https://news.google.com/newspapers?nid=1310&dat=19761226&id=zu5X-AAAAIBAJ&sjid=JOgDAAAAIBAJ&pg=6682,7182810&hl=en.

p. 34, "Don't ... it!" "Atari 2600: Don't Watch TV, Play It! 1970's Commercial." YouTube video, 0:30. April 16, 2014, www.youtube.com/watch?v=16zXSWac-8Q.

p. 35, "As ... black." Hardawar, Devindra. "Jerry Lawson, a Self-Taught Engineer, Gave Us Video Game Cartridges," Engadget, February 20, 2015, http://www.engadget.com/2015/02/20/jerry-lawson-game-pioneer.

p. 36, "The ... master." *Video Games: The Movie*. Directed by Jeremy Snead. Dallas, Texas: Mediajuice Studios, 2014. Netflix.

CHAPTER FOUR

p. 48, "video ... hazard." "AROUND THE NATION; Surgeon General Sees Danger in Video Games." *New York Times*, November 10, 1982, http://www.nytimes.com/1982/11/10/us/around-the-nation-surgeon-general-sees-danger-in-video-games.html.

p. 55, "Only ... compete." Schiesel, Seth. "Resistance Is Futile," *New York Times*, May 25, 2008, http://www.nytimes.com/2008/05/25/arts/television/25schi.html?pagewanted=print&_r=0.

p. 57, "Women ... revolution." "'Lady Arcaders' and Ms. Pac-Man's Significance in Women's Video Gaming," History Bandits, November 25, 2015, http://thehistorybandits.com/2015/11/25/lady-arcaders-and-ms-pac-mans-significance-in-womens-video-gaming.

CHAPTER FIVE

p. 62, "hundred ... phones." Batchelor, Bob, ed. *American Pop: Popular Culture Decade by Decade, 1990–Present*. Westport, CT: Greenwood Press, 2009.

p. 62–63, "Genesis ... Nintendon't." Rolfe, James. "SNES vs. Sega Genesis," Cinemassacre video, 26:45. August 17, 2012, http://cinemassacre.com/2012/08/17/snes-vs-sega-genesis-full-video.

p. 70, "*Doom* ... violence." Block, Jerald J., MD. "Lessons from Columbine: Virtual and Real Rage," *American Journal of Forensic Psychiatry*, Vol. 28, Issue 2, 2007, http://www.forensicpsychonline.com/Block.pdf.

p. 71, "theory ... instead." Campbell, Colin. "Do Violent Video Games Actually Reduce Real-World Crime?" *Polygon*, September 12, 2014, http://www.polygon.com/2014/9/12/6141515/do-violent-video-games-actually-reduce-real-world-crime.

CHAPTER SIX

p. 87, "As ... games." The Entertainment Software Association website, accessed December 27, 2015, http://www.theesa.com.

Glossary

applications (apps) Programs designed to provide a specific service or experience. For example, an app may allow the user to play a game, talk to friends, find directions on a map, or perform calculations.

arcade An entertainment business that provides its guests with a variety of games to play. Most of these games require coins to operate.

artificial intelligence The ability of a computer program to think, reason, or learn in the process of solving a problem.

cartridge In video games, a case holding game information. The case is made to be inserted into a specific game console.

communist A person or group of people who support the idea that the government should control goods and services.

computer processor A component in a computer that performs calculations or manipulates data.

computer programming A process in which a person writes instructions, known as code, for a computer to read and follow.

game console A system that allows a person to play video games on a television set.

game mechanics The rules or methods that allow players to interact with a game environment.

genre A category of movie, book, video game, or other art form. All of the items in this category share certain characteristics.

graphics In video games, visuals that a computer generates in real time.

inflation A slow increase in the cost of goods and services over time.

joystick A lever used as a controller in a video game or on a computer.

massively multiplayer online (MMO) A type of game that allows many people to play at the same time, in the same virtual world, over the Internet.

patent A document that protects the rights of an inventor to make and use their invention.

prosperity Being successful, usually financially.

role-playing game (RPG) A game in which players take on the persona of a fictional character or characters and participate in a story. These games often employ a fantasy or science fiction setting.

virtual Existing in a computer and not in physical reality.

Further Information

BOOKS

Griffiths, Devin C. *Virtual Ascendance: Video Games and the Remaking of Reality*. Lanham, MD: Rowman & Littlefield Publishing Group, 2013.

Harris, Blake J. *Console Wars: Sega, Nintendo, and the Battle that Defined a Generation*. New York: HarperCollins Publishers, 2014.

Hulick, Kathryn. *The Economics of a Video Game*. The Economics of Entertainment. New York: Crabtree Publishing Company, 2014.

Kent, Steven. *The Ultimate History of Video Games: From Pong to Pokémon—The Story Behind the Craze That Touched Our Lives and Changed the World*. New York: Three Rivers Press, 2001.

Stanton, Richard. *A Brief History of Video Games*. Philadelphia: Running Press, 2015.

FILMS

Indie Game: The Movie. Netflix, 2012.

Video Games: The Movie. Netflix, 2014.

WEBSITES

Entertainment Software Association
www.theesa.com
The ESA provides statistics on people's video game playing habits and on the video game industry.

Steam
steamcommunity.com
Steam is the most popular online destination for buying and playing computer games. Gamers on Steam have their own community.

The Strong: National Museum of Play
www.museumofplay.org
This museum showcases the history of play, including toys and video games.

Bibliography

Batchelor, Bob, ed. *American Pop: Popular Culture Decade by Decade, 1960–1989*. Westport, CT: Greenwood Press, 2009.

—, ed. *American Pop: Popular Culture Decade by Decade, 1990–Present*. Westport, Connecticut: Greenwood Press, 2009.

Griffiths, Devin C. *Virtual Ascendence: Video Games and the Remaking of Reality*. Lanham, MD: Rowman & Littlefield Publishing Group, 2013.

Hulick, Kathryn. *The Economics of a Video Game*. Economics of Entertainment. New York: Crabtree Publishing Company, 2014.

June, Laura. "For Amusement Only: The Life and Death of the American Arcade." *The Verge*, January 16, 2013. http://www.theverge.com/2013/1/16/3740422/the-life-and-death-of-the-american-arcade-for-amusement-only.

Lien, Tracy. "No Girls Allowed." *Polygon*, December 2, 2013. http://www.polygon.com/features/2013/12/2/5143856/no-girls-allowed.

Lule, Jack. *Understanding Media and Culture: An Introduction to Mass Communication*. Washington, DC: Flat World Education, Inc, 2015. http://www.saylor.org/site/textbooks/Understanding%20Media%20and%20Culture.pdf.

McGonigal, Jane. "Gaming Can Make a Better World." Filmed February 2010. TED video, 20:03. http://www.ted.com/talks/jane_mcgonigal_gaming_can_make_a_better_world?language=en.

Stanton, Richard. *A Brief History of Video Games*. Philadelphia: Running Press, 2015.

Video Games: The Movie. Directed by Jeremy Snead. Dallas, TX: Mediajuice Studios, 2014. Netflix.

Index

Page numbers in **boldface** are photographs. Entries in **boldface** are glossary terms.

About the Author

KATHRYN HULICK is a freelance writer, editor, and former Peace Corps volunteer. She has written numerous science articles and science news stories for children's magazines and websites. Her book *The Economics of a Video Game* came out in 2014. She enjoys hiking, gardening, painting, and playing video games with her husband, Steve, who has worked as a game programmer. He provided valuable assistance with the research for this book. They live in Massachusetts with their son and dog.